I love you more than ...

By Tagore Ramoutar

I love you more than ...

Big Bear!

I love you more than ...

a sausage roll!

I love you more than ...

Ella Grey Rabbit!

I love you more than ...

a pork pie!

I love you more than ...

a fresh juicy apple
straight from the tree!

I love you more than ...

Mimi Cuddly Dog!

I love you more than ...

a banana!

I love you more than ...

clouds in the blue sky!

I love you more than ...

carrot cake!

I love you more than ...

Scratch and Susie!

I love you more than ...

chocolate birthday cake!

I love you ...

totally, completely

and always!
XOXOX
(kiss cuddle kiss cuddle kiss)

First Published 2011.
Published by Longshot Ventures Ltd, UK. Copyright Tagore
Ramoutar, Longshot Ventures Ltd.

Printed in the UK: ISBN 978-1-907837-39-5.
Printed by Amazon: ISBN 978-1-907837-80-7.

www.ingramcontent.com/pod-product-compliance
Lightning Source LLC
Chambersburg PA
CBHW042110040426
42448CB00002B/205